Turning Pennies to Profits

How to Make $2000 - $4000 Every Month Selling Physical Books on Amazon FBA from Thrift Stores, Garage Sales and Flea Markets!

Copyright © 2015

All rights reserved. No part of this book may be reproduced in any form without permission in writing from the author. Reviewers may quote brief passages in reviews.

Disclaimer

No part of this publication may be reproduced or transmitted in any form or by any means, mechanical or electronic, including photocopying or recording, or by any information storage and retrieval system, or transmitted by email without permission in writing from the publisher.

While all attempts and efforts have been made to verify the information held within this publication, neither the author nor the publisher assumes any responsibility for errors, omissions, or opposing interpretations of the content herein.

This book is for entertainment purposes only. The views expressed are those of the author alone, and should not be taken as expert instruction or commands. The reader of this book is responsible for his or her own actions when it comes to reading the book.

Adherence to all applicable laws and regulations, including international, federal, state, and local governing professional licensing, business practices, advertising, and all other aspects of doing business in the US, Canada, or any other jurisdiction is the sole responsibility of the purchaser or reader.

Neither the author nor the publisher assumes any responsibility or liability whatsoever on the behalf of the purchaser or reader of these materials.

Any received slight of any individual or organization is purely unintentional.

Table of Contents

Introduction

Chapter 1 - How to Go Lucrative Selling Physical Books Online

Chapter 2- How FBA Works

Chapter 3- Earn Over $2000 Each Month Selling Books

Chapter 4- How to earn Thousands With Vintage and Seasonal Books

Chapter 5 - Increasing Trade on Amazon FBA using Simple IT tools

Conclusion

Bonus Chapter: 7 Steps to Success and Utilizing the Full Platform

Introduction

I want to thank you and congratulate you for downloading the book, Amazon FBA: How to make $2000 - $4000 Every Month Selling Physical Books on Amazon FBA from Thrift Stores, Garage Sales and Flea Markets!

This book contains proven steps and strategies for enabling you make up to $4000 in profits every month. The book takes you through the steps you need to take to be a seller on Amazon FBA, and then shows you what you need to do to earn yourself a minimum of $2000 month in, month out. The content in the book will surprise you when you see how much wealth you can make from a meager capital input of almost nil.

It is also gratifying to note that you do not need to be physically involved in the selling process of your books. However, this book guides you on how to put simple but important safeguards in place to ensure you reap the most from the business opportunity provided by Amazon FBA. It lists and explains the technical tools at your disposal that you have the freedom to choose from, to help you monitor the activity in your Amazon FBA account, including the movement of your inventory.

If you take the time to read this book fully and apply the information held within this book, it will help you to generate a voluminous guaranteed income in the range of $2000 and more every month.

Thanks again for downloading this book, I hope you enjoy it!

Chapter 1

How to Go Lucrative Selling Physical Books Online

Do flashes of a sweaty workforce at your workshop, go-down or boutique cross your mind when you hear *physical products*? Well, sometimes it is inevitable, and that is one of the reasons many people avoid committing to selling physical products online. They think: I began to sell online so I do not have to buy distribution vans or deal with a long line of distributors, who are sometimes unreliable and occasionally sluggish. Would I really wish to go back to that same hassle?

Now, here is some good news. You can go on enjoying all the convenience of getting your product known online, even in the case of your books, and still sell your physical products via the net without cutting a sweat. In fact, you will not even need to have a personal distribution workforce. You will still sell your physical books and make an incredibly huge margin.

So then this is true about selling physical products?

- That it is not any harder to sell physical products than it is to sell otherwise?
- That it is not mandatory to have massive amounts of money in order to purchase inventory in order to start my business?
- That I shall not have to face hurdles of managing physical inventory?
- That I shall not have to deal with fussy customers?
- That the market for physical products is actually not saturated?
- That I can even make better business selling physical products online than I can while trying to earn affiliate income?

Sure – that is all true. There have been numerous misconceptions about selling physical products via the net, but once you understand that they all add up to the myth of not understanding the opportunities that exist, you will be ready to welcome your monthly thousands of dollars with a smile. In fact, for those who learnt the ropes sometime ago, earning up to $4000 per month, and $2000 when the month is not so great is not a big deal.

So, what are the real facts on selling physical products online?

For one, you do not have to do anything as the product owner, besides committing your item. How, exactly, does that take place? Well, simple: you just outsource the service at every stage – easy.

- You can get marketable inexpensive items to make up your inventory, thus confirming the fact that you do not have to have loads of cash to begin your online business.
- Very many people are looking to buy physical items online on a daily basis, and this confirms that the market is not saturated; and instead, it is growing bigger.
- You can get ways of starting your online business with minimal or no capital at all.
- That going affiliate is not as lucrative as selling physical products.
- That you can make everything very easy and convenient for you by letting Amazon to do the selling for you.

What we are going to pursue now is that last point on Amazon. Why go anywhere else when Amazon has the FBA package that offloads you of any physical and mental burden and you just watch your money flow in?

Incidentally, FBA aptly stands for *Fulfillment by Amazon*. Does a customer want your product delivered? Amazon does it. The customer needs something, let us say – swapped? Amazon still straightens that out nicely. You need to see the money because you are in business? You just look at your Amazon account. Is there excess inventory sitting around with Amazon? No problem – Amazon can divert it to eBay; after all what you want is the money. How more convenient can it get?

Chapter 2

How FBA Works

How, for the love of a great profit, does this platform, FBA work? That must be something you are wondering, considering the market always seems competitive, and sometimes murky. Luckily, you are going to find all the necessary steps here, simply put and explicitly dealt with. Here are the main aspects that will reassure you about FBA:

1. Sending your inventory to an FBA center

Oh, oh... How do I do that? Well, no need to panic because that is very easy. You just get your shipment ready, of course, with the basic information including your address. Amazon will then consider the category of your product; its size; and such other minor but important details, and then determine the FBA center suited for your inventory. In fact, as soon as you complete the initial move, you will be able to see the destination address for your inventory.

That sounds easy – not much of a hassle and I know where my goods are...

But how safe is my inventory?

It is understandable that you should be concerned about the security of your products because you do not want your stuff lost, pilfered or delivered anywhere without guarantee for payment. That is why in these centers run by Amazon, you are assured of:

- Presence of security staff 24/7
- Storage of your products in very secure cages

Computerized order tracking that is automated; hence, it is free from manipulation.

Is there any special packaging required?

Well, Amazon would like your products to be well packaged to keep them safe from adverse elements. Just so you are sure that you are doing it right, and for convenience, you could purchase the packaging material right from Amazon. The material includes suitable poly bags; boxes; stretch wrap; bubble wrap; among other items.

Storage

Apart from the aspect of security that you have already been assured of, you need to know the following as well:

- That Amazon scans your products immediately on arrival and officially receives them at your designated FBA center.

- That Amazon takes the measurements for your products and records them accordingly, in order to get apt storage for them.

- That Amazon maintains a modern integrated system that allows you to monitor the movement of your inventory.

Your inventory at the FBA centers is conspicuous

Is that really possible? Well, that you might wonder because you are possibly imagining your products in a go-down. Well, with the FBAs, it would not really matter if your products were in a bunker or some other deeper zone. Amazon offers you ways of letting potential customers know that your products exist and that they are available for sale.

Is that not great! How does that happen?

Well, Amazon has offers for buyers as well, and that includes opportunities to acquire other products at a discount as they purchase their chosen products. So, in the process, your product stands a good chance of being seen by potential customers. This usually happens through:

i) The Buy Box

ii) Amazon Prime

iii) Free Super Saver Delivery

Do these platforms really work – you may wonder? And yes; they do work. In the UK, for example, sellers who use the FBA have reported an 85% sales increment. Others who do not care to go for special facilities but just join the FBA fraternity have had sales increments of

20% and upwards. You see with FBA, even customers who initially did not have your product in mind get to see it and get enticed to add it into their shopping cart. And so your sales keep rising without you incurring any extra cent.

Amazon is responsible for delivering your products

Really that happens? A customer makes an order and I do not have to do anything but wait for the payment? Well, it is one of those things that are as good as they sound. In fact, all across the countries in the European Union (EU) and the UK, you do not need to worry about making deliveries. The great Amazon sees to it that all products ordered from their FBA centers get to the customers in good time and in great shape.

Amazon saves you the problem of language barrier

When you are doing the selling personally, you are bound to have a language issue when you are English speaking and you want to sell to a Spanish speaking customer and so on. But Amazon is a global operator that deals with customers using their local languages. Do you see now that you will be able to reach a global populace more easily when selling via FBA centers than when you are selling through other avenues that are as limited as you are?

That is truly wonderful! You now want to begin selling your physical books through Amazon FBA.

This is how to begin the FBA business:

- Of course you have an account on Amazon; and if you do not, you are going to open one

- Now click *Inventory*.

- Then go to *Manage Inventory*

- Ask yourself: Which product do I want to sell through FBA? Once you have identified the product, click to tick against it within the column on the left

- Look at the drop down menu at *Actions*, and click against 'Change to Fulfilled by Amazon'.

- On the page that follows, do click *Convert*
- The rest of the directions are straightforward and your product henceforth appears on the FBA listing.

Chapter 3

Earn Over $2000 Each Month Selling Books

Did you know the reason many people do not buy your great product is that they do not know it exists? Oh yes! You take your book to a distributor who treats it like it was a prescription drug awaiting a Doctor's note. That is one major reason you need to choose an avenue like FBA where any customer who knocks to buy something has the opportunity to see your title.

As we have mentioned earlier, all you need is to enroll on the packages provided by Amazon and your product pops up whenever a customer is buying something on Amazon.

Then, of course, you need to cut your costs in order that, like a prudent business person, you maximize your profits. So, you have landed the right place – Amazon FBA – and you have your books available for sale. What is the starting point?

i) Be shrewd and offer some for free

Oh my goodness! You are wondering if your books will now go to charity… No – that is not the intention. The plan is to send word out that you have titles that are irresistible; titles worth reading. And you need that. As a buyer, once you like something and your mouth is drooling, you will not give a care how high the price is. But in contrast, it is common to hesitate to spend even a fraction of a dollar when you doubt if the book is worth reading.

And that is precisely the case with many people. So, as you offer free issues at the beginning, it is a way of entertaining feedback. With positive feedback, you can trust FBA to churn out your books like hot cakes. In fact, you could give out free books worth $1000 for starters, just for example, and have those attract positive feedback that becomes the greatest trigger for your income stream of over $2000 per month.

ii) Look out for great price offers while sourcing

When you are sourcing books to resell, you need to be conscious of the pricing. You surely want to leave yourself a reasonable margin even after offering a competitive price on Amazon. Some of the best sources of books for resale include garage sales; flea markets; and even thrift stores. Here you can buy at a fifth of the price at which you are going to sell at Amazon FBA, while still keeping them affordable.

Here are some tricks you could use:

- Do your spying before your buying day so that you can compare the prices in a particular store with elsewhere

- Monitor the stores to identify the days when they have special sales. Then time the last day of that sales period – you are bound to buy good books in bags for a song

- Monitor the operations of the libraries within your vicinity. You are likely to find great sales and relatively low number of buyers. This is because local libraries do not usually take their sales advertising far. So the shrewd bookseller that you are, you could make a kill for such sales simply because demand is relatively low.

iii) Look far and wide for cheap sourcing

Cheap selling stores around your hometown are not the only places you could buy books from. How about checking out the expansive Amazon market and establishing the titles that are on high demand. Then check out eBay – no restrictions, mark you; just some business acumen. If you find that those same titles are available for sale at eBay, do the math. If you can buy a title at eBay and sell it via FBA at a good margin, why hesitate? You will be hastening your move to clinching your monthly $4000.

iv) Repent and refresh your thinking

Nothing spiritual here, but you surely need to forgive yourself for having wasted precious time limiting your chances of success on Amazon. Those myths you have held onto thinking they were Gospel truths have cost you book profits you could have earned in their thousands. From now onwards, try and learn the actual facts of selling through FBA, and leave your mind open for creative thinking. A sale is a sale is a sale: you do not have to follow any book or even any conventions. The following are non-truths you need to discard:

- That selling a book below $10 will not make you reasonable profits. Hello! What is reasonable? The last time I checked, really, it took a penny and another and another to pile up to a dollar. So how else would you expect to accumulate $2000 each month or thereabouts than by leaving your pricing open and liberal?

- That you are not allowed to indicate your book is new unless you are the publisher. Really? Where did you get that? Someone's thinking on face book? Well, it is not correct. Think about it this way – When you tell us you have a new set of China, is it because you were part of the pottery group? Surely no. It only means the item is unused; not old; as good as direct from the shop.

- That you can only earn handsome profits by selling textbooks on Amazon. Oh, no – that, again, is pure imagination. Any book – that is, any – will stand a chance of selling on FBA. The factors that determine whether a customer will buy a book or not as often as varied as potential customers are. So, if you are serious about making a kill on Amazon FBA, add to your titles every time you have a chance.

    Remember your inventory is safe at the FBA stores, so there is no need to worry. Besides, you could always recall your items if you wanted any day.

v) Focus on prudent sourcing and interesting choices

Take your time hunting for comparatively low prices, particularly from garage sales. An individual who is putting up a garage sale does not want to return any stuff to the garage. A garage sale is very different from a sale in a store because a store could wait an eternity to get a good price for the items, but an individual with a garage sale wants to be through fast – often the same day.

So you are likely to buy books in a garage sale for prices that will leave your mouth agape – well, not literally, as you do not want to show the seller that you are super impressed... Possibly, you will still be pushing for some bigger bargain as is the nature of merchants...

In fact, in garage sales, you are likely to come across unique books, and possibly gather some history associated with them from the book owners, that you could use to market the books on Amazon FBA.

For example, while I do not expect to hear of a garage sale at the White House or Buckingham Palace because things there are more for Public than Private interest, imagine garage sales for heirs of confidants of famous people. You could source a book from such homes and sell them for a fortune on Amazon FBA!

vi)   Sell all and sundry

The most prudent thing is to sell any title you find in good shape. After all, how would you know a book is not going to sell well unless you test the waters? And for that single book that you have never come across before, how can you tell, anyway, if it is the title to transform your life on FBA? The fact that selling at Amazon FBA is so cost-effective, should encourage you to sell as many titles as possible, and also capitalize on low shipping cost by shipping out large bulks to FBA centers.

Chapter 4

How to earn $'000s on Vintage and Seasonal Books

Think of Sinbad the Sailor, Gulliver's Travels and such other books of old, and see how much nostalgia they elicit just hearing those names! And you know most of those stories have been retold again and again, adding some spice here and some more there. But to get the original story is often very difficult. So if you have a copy in your house and it is intact, it could fetch you a healthy sum on Amazon FBA.

Here are the best areas of focus:

- **Ancient books that are still in readable shape**

If you want to fetch great prices, do not concentrate on heaps and heaps of the same title – no. Instead, be selective and find those titles that are rare to find.

- **Seek out-of-print books**

For one, anyone who wants to see material as original as it was will not be deterred by pricing. So, as long as you have a copy still in good shape, feel confident to sell it through Amazon FBA.

- **Have a go at reference manuals**

Think of collectors, possibly of vintage vehicles, who refurbish those cars for special competitions or just for fun. Would such a guy not find a Ford repair manual from the early 1900s extremely dear? Whereas the Ford Company has obviously modified the Ford brand to something very different from the original one, the manuals of the original brand must be of great interest to some people.

- **Go for books that can be given out as gifts**

Do you not think, for instance, that a Cinderella book of old might fascinate a young girl if she received the book from her grandma?

- **Capitalize on pricing**

After you have done what you need to do to establish your name on Amazon, set a profitable price for your product. The free shipping offered by FBA usually makes buyers ignore the apparently high pricing. That allows you to earn high margins just because the platform makes delivery easy, convenient and cheap for the customer.

- **Capitalize on seasons to sell relevant books**

The fact that Amazon FBA sells and makes deliveries 24/7 enables you to sell books that are trending at a particular time even when the demand may not have been predictable. For example, you could send a history book to FBA soon following a coup in a country, calculating that the interest created in the country over the coup could lead to sales. All you need is be vigilant and creative, and FBA's platform will facilitate great sales - $2000 to $4000 per month will not be a mirage but a reality.

- **Make use of variety**

Since storage is not a handicap, you will hike your chances of selling more when you have more titles available to customers. When this type of book is low in sales, another one could be on high demand. In fact, the chances of having more than one or two titles selling well concurrently are very high when you have many different books listed on Amazon FBA.

- **Riding on the credibility of FBA**

You do not have to price your books for a song. Compared to other sites, your books will still sell in great numbers even when your price is higher because the customers are confident of timely deliveries and friendly conditions. They know that if a wrong delivery is made or the book has something missing like a page, a refund or a swap will not be a big deal.

Generally speaking, you just need to be experimental and think outside the box. If you concentrate on contemporary books that everyone else is offering, you may earn yourself just normal profits. But you want to have a range of $2000 to $4000 every single month, so you need to be ingenious in your offers.

In fact, one blogger tells of how he purchased a printer toner for a dollar and within 48hrs he had disposed of it online at close to $40. In essence, earning very many times more your purchase price if you sourced your items from garage sales, thrift stores or flea markets is the norm.

Why do many online customers prefer FBA?

i) There is the shipping arrangement that often gives the customer an opportunity through Free Super Saver Shipping and also Amazon Prime.

ii) There is a very wide range of products – including some that are unique, rare and dear – and that fascinates many customers.

iii) Many customers are able to find bonus items on FBA because there are many sellers who offer samples for free to draw attention and gain feedback.

iv) The storage service offered by Amazon FBA attracts many sellers including those that sell in bulk.

Chapter 5

Increasing Trade on Amazon FBA using Simple IT tools

You want a smooth sales process whatever you are selling – true? Sure. So, even when it comes to selling physical books on Amazon FBA, definitely you would like a smooth process that culminates in enviably great profits. When we are targeting a monthly income of between $2000 and $4000, you cannot afford at all to ignore any tool that brings any positive contribution.

You want your consignment to be well labeled before shipping; correctly charged according to proposed rates; and you also want to be able to monitor the up and down sliding of your stock level. For you, an ambitious trader, of course, you are not going to talk of five or so titles and a carton or two of their copies. You are going to talk of a long list of titles and possibly tons of copies of those titles; thus the need for keen and accurate handling of your business at every stage. In modern day, you will concur that the best way to go about it is automating things and using appropriate technology.

In that regard, below is a list of tools you could use to help you maintain your steady flow of income from FBA:

1) Listing Tools

There is a wide variety of tools you could choose from to list your books on Amazon FBA. And why would you need special tools when Amazon provides Seller Central? Here is why:

- Putting up all your inventory on Amazon becomes faster
- Putting labels on your product, the book, becomes more convenient also
- Putting up prices, and adjusting them when there is need, is also easier and more convenient

- When you are targeting an income of $2000 and beyond each month, you must be handling big inventory, probably 50 items and more every month. So you, definitely, need a modern and suitable listing tool.

The most common of the tools include:

a) ASellerTool

This one helps you scan your books and list them and it is fairly priced, considering that both services are somewhat packaged together saving you tens of dollars in the meantime. Expect to enjoy a week of free trial, which is a big plus because you will be sure you like how it works before you pay a cent. It sells for around $30.

b) Listtee

This listing tool is relatively easy to use and it produces very clear screenshots. While it sells for around $40, it does offer a 2-week free trial period.

Bonus: This tool also has a version – Pro Version – that also comes with a scouting tool.

c) Neatoscan

This is a multi-purpose tool. Of course it does the listing pretty well; but it also does some inventory control. For example, every book that sells is cancelled out by this particular tool. And you are not restricted to Amazon FBA. Rather, you can still use it on eBay or even Half.

Uniqueness: What providers of this tool do is, sort of, partner with you. Instead of offering the tool for a dear price, they opt to charge you some commission only when you make a sale – sounds fair. So, for every book sale that you make on FBA, they pick between 1% and 3% of the sales price. Of course, it also gives you a trial period: 2wks.

d) Scan Power

This is a listing too that provides you room to include fundamental information that helps you in making sales decisions along the way. For example, you can include the cost of the product and the current price that you have chosen. At the same time, you could give yourself a limit beyond which you are not going to take your price. In such a case each time you effect a change in selling price, your tool prompts you if you are crossing the line. The tool also updates you on the level of your inventory remaining at the FBA centers.

Listing up to 1000 items every month is no big deal with this tool; it remains efficient even in retrieving the additional information on added product notes and so on. This tool also offers you a 2wk trial period, after which you pay a monthly fee of around $40.

e) SellerEngine Plus

This one is quite robust but somewhat complex to use. It offers you a month of free trial, but after that, you are called upon to pay a monthly fee of around $50.

2) Scouting Tools

These are tools that assist in identifying suitable inventory that you could buy for resale. Some of these tools are the same that have the listing function. Some of those with the double function include:

- ASellerTool
- Listtee
- Neatoscan
- Scan Power

Others with a strictly scouting function include:

a) Book Scouter

Though being placed here as a scouting tool, it is actually a tool that you use on bookscouter.com to search for the best prices being offered by particular buyers. All you do is type in the book's ISBN and stores and pricing come up. This tool is popular with students seeking to sell back books that they no longer need.

It is important to note that unless you are planning to recall some of your books from Amazon FBA and sell them via bookscouter.com, you surely may not need this tool for your operations at FBA.

b) Profit Bandit

This is a scouting tool meant for the Smartphone and it goes for around $15. That buying price is a one-off and it does not call for any monthly fees. It enables you to consolidate plenty of information to utilize in the future; like,

- Source of the item/physical book
- Condition of the item/book
- The price you paid for the item
- The total units you bought
- The item's selling price at Amazon FBA
- The profit you are set to make for each item after netting off Amazon's charges.

c) Scout Pal

This basically works well on PDAs and Smartphones. If you use it, you will be able to see book prices from a site like Abe Books. The tool offers you a week of free trial and thereafter you are called upon to subscribe monthly at around $10 per month.

3) Re-pricing Tools

You are a good marketer, undoubtedly, and as such you will find it necessary to review your book prices periodically in order to take advantage of upcoming favorable conditions and also to cushion yourself from a lull occasioned by unfavorable market conditions.

Considering this, having a convenient tool to facilitate price amendments is an advantage. Here below, are some of the popular tools:

a) NeatoScan

b) For this tool, the function of modifying prices is integrated with the Inventory Manager; so the tool seems to have a duo purpose.

c) RepriceIt

This is a good price resetting tool that does not limit the number of times you alter your prices. It also updates your base records accordingly in a way that you will not have to do a thing once you alter particular prices. It is also a tool that does not limit how you make your modifications: you can change prices for some items while leaving others intact.

The amount you pay for this tool depends on the size of your inventory. Whenever your inventory is within 500-item range downwards, your pay is around $10; then the price hikes as your inventory goes up. Something else you will like about this tool is that it gives you room to alter prices for up to a hundred thousand products – how great!

Sellery

This is a sophisticated too that, though easy to use, seems to target big scale sellers. You may need it as you continue to blossom in your business, because it will enable you to modify your prices in different FBA centers simultaneously. In fact, you can even integrate it with the system in your physical store somewhere.

Another good feature with this tool is that it enables you to set a minimum price. This, obviously, guards against you setting a price that falls below the cost of your goods. As a serious entrepreneur, you need to break even on every single item; at least, if nothing else.

The price of this tool is reasonable if you are a big seller and you optimize its use. You are called upon to pay a minimum of $100 every month, or a fee equivalent to 1% of your monthly sales, whichever is higher. That, however, is preceded by a period of 2wks free trial.

Conclusion

Thank you again for downloading this book!

I hope this book was able to help you to see how easy it is to earn thousands of dollars every month selling books. I hope it has given you the motivation you need to begin your own online business, selling books that you could source for a song in your neighborhood or from online shops.

The next step is to open an Amazon FBA account and begin the process of piling up book stocks for shipping to FBA centers.

Finally, if you enjoyed this book, please take the time to share your thoughts and post a review on Amazon. It'd be greatly appreciated!

Thank you and good luck!

Bonus Chapter: 7 Steps to Success

Taking that first leap into owning your own business can seem a bit overwhelming at first, however you can be sure that you will be opening all of the right doors if you follow the guidelines set forth in this book. Here are 7 steps to make sure that you make the most of your money and find yourself swiftly on the path to earning your financial independence and security. You can take your future into your own hands, and these guidelines can help you get there even faster!

Step 1: Find the Proper Niche for Yourself

The first step that you have to take when you decide to start owning your personal financial success is to decide what exactly you want, and what kind of things you want to sell online. You will want to pick something that you can turn a good profit with and that isn't already flooding the market. So, how can you find just the right niche on Amazon?

Make sure that you put some thought into choosing the proper niche and take the time to plan out what exactly you want to sell; be very careful not to just pick something esoteric that you like, but that others would not really be into. Remember, you want to make money from this venture, not show off an eccentric hobby that you might have. With that being said:

Choose an item that you will enjoy marketing and that you are knowledgeable about, or that you wouldn't mind learning about. Even though it is important to sell an item that others will actually purchase, you should still make sure that you can find enjoyment in it as well, so that you can effectively market it.

Do some market research and make sure that your potential customers are actually searching for the product that you are considering placing for sale on Amazon. It's important that you are filling a need online because there are so many listings and places to shop that you want to move into an area that isn't already being inundated with tons of competition. Of course, you will always have some competitors; however, you can start off on the right foot by not trying to go into a market that already has a huge list of sellers.

In the midst of your market research, you should also make sure that not only are shoppers searching for your potential product, but that they are spending their money on it, as well. You want people to not only be excited about information on your items, but to be interested enough that they are willing to spend their disposable income on them.

You should also make sure that there is at least a little bit of competition already existing on the market for your products. This will help you generate more interest in the things that you want to sell online. People are much more likely to want something that they think that others want, as well.

Another thing that you should consider when you are trying to decide what niche you would be interested in filling on the Amazon marketplace is whether or not your potential product will be something that people want to buy for a long period. For instance, if you are trying to market something that is only specific to a certain time of year, or to a holiday, then you can't expect to keep making money off of your inventory for the rest of the year.

Make sure that you aren't going to be investing more in your product than you can make from it when you sell it online. You want to be able to buy low and then have enough interest generated in your products that you can sell high and turn a tidy little profit for yourself.

Don't choose an item that can be easily purchased from one of the big name stores. If a customer can go to a store and pick up what you are selling with ease, then they are much more likely to go that route. Instead, try to choose something that is a little more on the specialty side without going too far into the esoteric.

When you are trying to determine the niche that you want to fill on Amazon, you should try to narrow your products down and be a little bit more specific in order to really draw in those customers. For instance, instead of just marketing watches for sale, try going a little deeper and selling engraved, silver pocket watches. This kind of thinking will help you get more quality shoppers that actually want to spend their money with you instead of people that are just browsing a large category of items online.

You should try to find an item to sell that is in between the $10 and $200 range. Anything that costs less than that is a lot harder for you to move, and anything higher takes a little more work to convince a shopper that they need it. In addition, you need to be careful that you don't fall into the trap of selling something that will require any kind of warranty or repair service, or something that has a lot of moving or motorized parts that could need repair. Plus, try to stay away from items that are extremely fragile so that you can reduce your risk of shipping damages or returns for something that is defective at the time of delivery.

Pay special attention to the quality of the items that you choose to sell, whether you are drop shipping them or purchasing them beforehand. Remember, the quality of the product that you choose to sell will reflect on you in either a positive or negative light, so do your best to provide something is well worth the amount of money that you are asking people to spend on it. When you sell something that is manufactured well you also get to rest assured knowing that you won't get as many returns or as many displeased customers.

This might seem like a lot of information about one small part of your new online business, but it is easily one of the most important decisions that you will be making when you are getting started. Without the right products to put up for sale, you will find yourself frustrated with your lack of success and you can cause your business to fail before you even get a chance to get going.

Step 2: Price Your Products in an Effective Manner

Once you have determined what types of products you want to sell using Amazon, you need to be able to price them in a way that allows you to maintain your overhead and still earn enough money to make your business worth your time. This aspect of your business should actually come into play while you are in the process of deciding what types of products to market to your internet shoppers. Make sure that you can sell the items that you have chosen for at least twice what you spend on them. This might sound extravagant, but once you start doing some shopping around you should be able to find a wholesale supplier that you can get your product from at a reasonable cost. This will allow you to provide a decent mark up on it and see your profits start growing even quicker.

When you are setting up your pricing structure, you need to take several things into consideration. Not only do you need to cover the cost of your actual products, you also need to look at the amount of money that you are spending on fees, marketing and advertising, plus the net income that you want to generate with your business every month. Sitting down with a budget is going to be one of the best things that you can do before you start off on your own. You need to crunch a few numbers to insure that you are pricing your items in the most effective way that you can.

It's important for you to do some research at this point in the game, as well. Look at the pricing of your particular product when it is sold by other shops or even on other venues. If everyone else is letting it go for $15 and you have to sell it at $20 in order to make a profit, then you need to go back to the first step and find something to list online that you can set a competitive price for while still making the money that you want to.

Step 3: Explore Drop Shipping

When you are looking through your budget, you might not like the idea of putting as much of your personal income into play before you start making more money. Fortunately, with FBA, this is a viable option for your new venture because you can easily set things up so that you drop ship your products to your customers. When you use drop shipping, it means that you don't actually own the items that you are listing for sale before you sell them to someone else.

The first thing that you need to do is find a company that works well with these methods and list their items for sale on Amazon at a higher price than they sell them for. After a customer makes a purchase from you, you pay the wholesale price for the item and it gets shipped to the shopper. Your profit can then be measured as the difference between the wholesale cost and the amount that you actually sold the product for. This can be a great way for you to get started without having to come up with a lot of capital, plus you don't have to worry about dealing with a whole bunch of items and trying to ship them and store them.

Step 4: Make Use of Your Reports

Setting up and using your seller account on the Amazon website is a pretty simple process. However, you should remember that it isn't a "set it and forget it" kind of thing. Amazon provides a whole host of different kinds of reports for you to be able to track everything that matters to you about your new business.

These reports can show you what kind of sales you are making and how often your products are being shipped to certain areas. This can help you decide whether or not you are making a bid for customers in the right way.

Not only can these reports help you determine whether or not you have a hot item that you are missing out on selling more of, they can also help you track your actual sales so that you can continue to maintain the same type of profit every month. They make it even easier for you to grow your profit, so don't overlook them!

Step 5: Pay Attention to Your Time

Even though you won't be clocking in and out in the traditional sense, it is still important that you keep track of the time that you spend on your online selling ventures. It is important to look at how much money you are earning based on how many hours that you are putting into the work. If you find that you aren't making good use of your days than you should look at adjusting things in your selling strategies so that you are bringing in more cash as opposed to spending more time. Remember, you are leaving the typical working world behind for a reason, so you don't want to find yourself chained to the same old time clock, but you do still want to get paid well for your work.

Step 6: Market Your Products and Advertise

One of the biggest things for you to keep in mind when you are trying to get your online business established is that you have got to advertise. It will not matter if you have the best product in the world for sale if no one ever knows about it. Your items might come up in searches, which will still give you some income, but in order to really capitalize on all of the customers that are out there, you have to learn how to market yourself in an effective way and really get your name out there.

Tell Everyone

You should try to make use of the very medium that you are selling on in order to advertise your products. The internet is filled with different ways for you to show people why you are the best option for them to shop with. Even if you don't have an actual online storefront, you can use things like social media sites and blogs to sell yourself. Don't just start throwing comments on different sites about the particular listing that you have for sale; go in depth a little bit. You can try setting up a blog and including an interesting article detailing a few facts about the item that you are trying to make visible and then provide a link so that your readers can purchase it, or you can set up a whole buzz revolving around it by using several different social media sites together to create a whole marketing structure.

Make Your Item Look Worthy

You should also be aware of how your item listing looks to other people. Make sure that you are honest and informative when it comes to the description that you write. In addition, it's important that you have very descriptive images to accompany it. Remember, online shoppers don't get to touch the items that they are considering purchasing, so your images can easily be said to make or break your sales. You wouldn't want to buy an item that has a terrible picture to show it off, so don't expect other people to do it either.

Take Advantage of Big Shopping Times

Even though you don't want all of your items to be seasonal in nature, you should pay attention to the different times of the year when your customers are gearing up for the holidays. People spend a lot more money on websites like Amazon during certain times of the year and it is definitely advisable to capitalize on this larger amount of traffic. You can either add in more items for sale in your listings to cater to the hot holiday items of the year or you can try something like running certain specials or sales in order to bring more purchases in.

Keywords are Important

If no one sees your item when they search for things that are similar to it, then you are not doing your job right, and you certainly are not going to make very sales. You should always make sure that your description makes good use of keywords and that you add in the right ones to make your product come up easily at the top of any search executed by your potential shoppers. This is one thing that can take you out of business early in the game if you don't get the hang of it pretty quickly, so just try to keep a close eye on it.

These are just suggestions on how to effectively market yourself and your listings on Amazon, but in order for you to be really successful you will have to learn to think in a creative manner when it comes to making your customers want to shop only with you. Don't be afraid of your marketing skills, or afraid to try something different.

Step 7: Treat People Right

It might seem like it goes without saying, but you would be surprised how often people disregard the massive impact that great customer service skills can have on the repeated success of your business ventures. You should always conduct yourself with professionalism and try to remember that you are the face of your business. You represent everything there is about it so you want to make sure that you act accordingly during any interactions that have. This not only means the service that you provide with customers but it also means that you should represent yourself in a professional manner with any other people you deal with, including Amazon associates or anyone else online.

All of these steps will be an integral part of making your online business a true success. If you follow them, along with the other information held in this guide then you will be sure to make more than $7,500 each and every month and you will never have to make money for anyone but yourself again. It has never been easier for you to make money from your own home and there is no reason why you can't be a part of the new generation of business owners by starting today!

www.ingramcontent.com/pod-product-compliance
Lightning Source LLC
LaVergne TN
LVHW092246250125
802182LV00006B/248